# High-Tech IDs

## FROM FINGER SCANS TO VOICE PATTERNS

# High-Tech IDs

## FROM FINGER SCANS TO VOICE PATTERNS

By Salvatore Tocci

**Franklin Watts**
A Division of Grolier Publishing
New York ■ London ■ Hong Kong ■ Sydney
Danbury, Connecticut

Photographs ©: AP/Wide World Photos: 29 (Bob Child), 88 (Peter Cosgrove), 13 (David Longstreath), 35 (Lennox McLendon), 27 (Alan Mothner), 15 right (Orlin Wagner), 15 left, 74, 77 (Alexander Zemlianichenko); Courtesy of Ultra-Scan Corporation: 99; Grace Davies Photography: 9, 53, 56, 66, 71; Liaison Agency Inc.: 79 (George De Keerle), 49 (Eric Bazin), 38 (Spencer Grant), 12 (Hulton Getty), 25; Millenium Jet Inc.: 101; Photo Provided by Recognition Systems: 31, 43; Photo Researchers: 52 (Danny Brass/Science Source), cover (James King-Holmes/SPL), 64 (Hank Morgan/Science Source), 82 (Sinclair Stammers/SPL); Shanin Leeming: 110.

Illustrations by George Stewart: 18; Bob Italiano: 20; and Mike DiGiorgio: 47.

Visit Franklin Watts on the Internet at:
http://publishing.grolier.com

Library of Congress Cataloging-in-Publication Data

Tocci, Salvatore.
    High-tech IDs: from finger scans to voice patterns / by Salvatore Tocci.
        p.  cm.
    Includes bibliographical references and index.
    Summary: Describes a variety of devices and systems used for identifying individuals, including finger and hand scans, iris and retinal scans, fingerprinting, DNA fingerprinting, and voice pattern recognition, and gives examples of how they are used.
    ISBN 0-531-11752-9 (lib. bdg.)                    0-531-16462-4 (pbk)
    1. Biometry Juvenile literature.  2. Identification Juvenile literature.  [1. Biometry.]  I. Title.
QH323.5.T63        2000
599.9'4—dc21                                                                    99-37380
                                                                                  CIP